CU00659653

Social Media and Teenager's Mental Health

TO WHAT EXTENT CAN SOCIAL MEDIA AFFECT THE
MENTAL HEALTH OF THE YOUTH?

Joyal Biju K.

Copyright © 2020 Joyal Biju K.

All rights reserved.

ISBN: 9798638494063

Acknowledgements

I would like to firstly thank God, who has helped me guide the right path into doing my research, without whom the research would have been incomplete.

*I wish to express my sincere gratitude to my supervisor, **Ms. Divya Sharma**, whose expertise, helped me to properly guide my research into the right track and helped me complete it. Without her persistent help and encouragement, the goal of this project would not have been completely realized.*

*I would like to pay my special regards to **Mr. Jerome Bernard**, the personal project coordinator, for all his helpful advices and persistent encouragement for the achievement of my project. Along with him, I would like to extend my gratitude to my resource person, **Mr. Thierry Dupuy**, who has given me most of the guidance and support that I have needed to properly conduct my research and achieve my goal of completing it successfully. I am also indebted to the Arc-en-Ciel International School committee for enabling me to conduct my researches on this topic.*

I would like to acknowledge the support of my family, who gave me wonderful inspirations and counsels based on my topic, and helped me improve my arguments and claims, by giving me solid real-life examples based on the topic. They kept me going on the right track, and without them, the research would have been incomplete.

I want to take this opportunity to thank all friends and colleagues who have contributed in the collection of data through the questionnaire, and also for their companionship and constant feedback that they have given me.

In addition, I want to extend my acknowledgements to all the authors and experts from research articles that I have referred to, based on the same theme, during my research.

Table of Contents

I. Introduction

Social media has enhanced mass communication facilities and has transformed our societies in a lot of ways, and its impacts are portrayed through our modern younger generations. There is no doubt that social media is slowly taking over various cultures and economies of our world of today, and due to this, children are slowly utilizing it for various uses. Social media can be defined as a platform where the transmission of ideas, thoughts and information are facilitated (DOLLARHIDE, 2019) and also where people get to advertise a product or even to find out trending global topics.

As the research question of this study is to outline the extent at which social media impacts the mental health of the youth, my research study aims to indicate the negative impacts of social media on the mental health of adolescents, and to avoid being controversial, to demonstrate its positive impacts on their psychological well-being. Companies such as Facebook, are encouraging the use of social media among the youth by helping them to keep in touch with friends and family, to figure out what's going on in the world, and to share and express what matters to them, according to their mission statement (Facebook Investor Relations, n.d.). There are also companies that extend the positive impacts of social media by portraying how it can help increase cognitive learning. However, there are also other groups and services, that try to reduce the usage of social media consumption among teenagers, while outlining its negative impacts.

This research study will firstly outline the positive impacts of social media on teenagers' mental health, and then it will explicit the negative impacts of social media on their psychological well-being and thus portray solutions to the youth, proposing ways on reducing their consumptions levels on various social media platforms. To do this, I plan on gathering data by conducting a questionnaire with various teachers based on their views about this topic as well as from the perspectives of a group of teenagers and thus comparing the data collected. Other sources will be derived from online sources and pre-made research reports on this similar topic.

This social media exploration study also intends to quote the works of specialists such as Niall McCrae, Jacob Amedie, Holly Michelle Rus and others, who also have researched and broadened the same theme compared to the one of this study.

II. Methodology

2.1. PRIMARY DATA

For this research, a questionnaire was conducted amongst 50 adolescents and 25 different teachers of the Arc-en-Ciel International School of Lomé, Togo, along with other global schools, to gain opinions based on the impacts of social media applications amongst teenagers. The researcher examined the phenomenon that was derived from the questionnaire, through clear observations in numerical representations and through statistical analysis, organized in spreadsheets and graphs.

By convenience, there is no exact research sampling method that was used, however out of all the classes in the school in the secondary program, the questionnaire was only sent to the classes ranged from 8th till 12th grade, because starting from 8th grade, most teenagers of the school are seen in that range. This pick for the questionnaire's recipients was necessary for data analysis for my research because it ties along with my target audience, which includes young adults, who are aged from 13 years and above. The opinion of teachers was sought in this research, to get their answers on how teenagers, using examples of their students in particular, on how social media affected young people's mental health.

The questionnaire was sent to the recipients through google forms, so that they could instantly take 2-4 minutes of their time to answer the questionnaire. It included ranges of questions between multiple choice questions, and choices between a linear scale. Also, an evaluation of the questionnaire was asked, to help me gain improvement areas amongst the questions. The questionnaire was the only primary data that was conducted for this research, and it is linked down in the appendix.

2.2. SECONDARY DATA

Within this topic of the influence of social media on teenager's mental health, there are a lot of secondary sources that can help guide the researchers gain background information on both the positive and negative sides of the story. This research included the usage of a vast number of secondary sources, including articles, websites, books, earlier studies, and many more. The criteria that were used to select the secondary sources included the type of source, whether the source either gave a positive view or a negative view about the topic, and whether the information was credible enough, compared to the research topic. The criteria used to sort the data was to find out the different views on the topic, both positive and negative sources, then distinguishing them in different compartments, to gain access to both types of sources, for the research analysis. Thus, to evaluate the sources, criteria such as its credibility, authenticity, author/ publisher, date of publishing, type of data, its purpose and consistency were determined before beginning to accurately incorporate them into the research.

III. Positive impacts of social media

Social media has been created, with the main purpose of improving communication amongst people across the globe, regardless of the distance between them, or other obstacles. However, the four main uses of social media can be derived from the acronym SLTM, in which S stands for Sharing information across platforms, accessible to a variety of global audiences, through broadcasting sites, news medias, such as YouTube; L stands for Learning information, for instance about global topics from communities around the world, and/ or about big live issues happening in the world; I stands for interacting with people all over the world, either by texting, through apps such as Facebook or twitter, or by talking face-to-face with people all over the world; and finally, M stands for Marketing, where social media is used for promoting ideas, products and events that are important to people (Thoughtful Learning, 2014).

Based on the questionnaire that I have given to the students and teachers, the positive effect of the usage of social media, is to mostly keep in touch with family, relatives, and family, and thus for research work. The data is presented in the bar charts below.

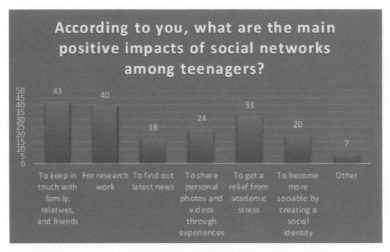

Chart 1: Main positive effect of social Media (Students Perspective)

Most students think that the main positive impact of social media usage is to keep in touch with other people, both people they know, and they do not know.

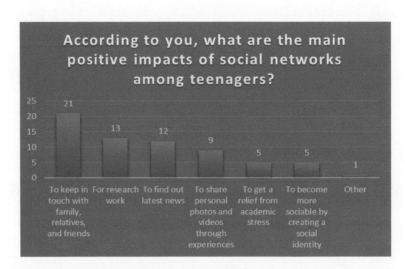

Chart 2: Main positive effect of social Media (Teachers Perspectives on Students)

Most teachers also think that the main positive impact of social media usage amongst teenagers is also to keep in touch with family, friends, and relatives, as well as for research work.

Due to these reasons, social media is now part of the modern-day society, acting as an indicator that is increasingly changing our world. It is particularly important to derive the benefits from social media on the mental health of youngsters, rather than always specifying its dangers, by discouraging young people from using it the right way.

3.1. EMPATHY

Social media has been around for quite a few years, and it has been growing due to various consumer demands. However, one of its main impacts, includes its impact on our recognition of empathy. The simple meaning of empathy ties around our broadened understanding and sharing of our feelings for others (Verywell Mind, 2019). Based on a data finding in Netherlands, amongst teens between 13 to 15 years of age, social media use was considered to increase cognitive empathy, by helping teens understand others' feelings, as well as to increase affective empathy, through the sharing of others' feelings. This study indicated a strength in the social skills between teenagers, due to social media usage, over a period of time (Social Media Use Increases Empathy For Peers, 2016).

Social media has an increasing impact on empathy in young people's minds and this is due to the lack of self-support and helps to offer a confidence boost in their lives. Matthew Oransky, an assistant professor of adolescent psychiatry at Mount Sinai Hospital in New York City and a practicing therapist, had previously said that many of his patients, commonly find social connections through social medias online, mostly when they are unable to find such support in real-life. He says that this is particularly achieved with adolescents, who fall in the LGBT societies, or other marginalized kids, such as kids in foster homes, or kids with serious illnesses (Jacewicz, 2017). Hereby, teens tend to create "supportive communities", via social media, to outline the contrasts between living in isolation, offline, or finding support online. Being empathetic, online, can mean a lot of things, because as we show our feelings for others, we get to tend to feel emotional and since social media allows us to easily communicate and find out global trending topics seamlessly, adolescents and all people in general, can show their support by donations, or just by a simple like and/or a positive comment. This can allow the transfer of companionship amongst teens, whilst feeling like there is somebody to talk to; emotional support, to receive advice and heartfelt messages, as well as total support, through facilities such as aid and any kind of help, when they are felt left out of societies. Due to the increase in scientific and technological innovations over the years, social media is enabling a "safer and more accessible way" to help teenagers connect with anyone across the globe, regardless of the location or any other boundaries, to share, learn and chat seamlessly. Due to this, most kids are able to evolve in their social spaces, and develop broader friendships, which in turn allows them to have more self-confidence, more social-support and increases their empathy for others that either fall in the safe society as they do, or to help another community that is in need.

3.2. SOCIALIZATION AND COMMUNICATION

Two researchers, Helen Vossen of Utrecht University and Patti Valkenburg of the University of Amsterdam, note that "understanding and sharing the emotions of others are crucial skills to develop in adolescence, as they greatly influence social interaction." (PACIFIC STANDARD STAFF, 2016). This is considered as a great benefit for the usage of social media in adolescents' lives because it gives them the opportunity to create a social identity, and make newer friends from diverse backgrounds, and to interact with them, around the globe in a safer and balanced way.

Socialization amongst teens can be engaged in many ways including knowing about worldwide topics, and raising charity donations for various local and global events, enhancing both individual and collective creativity as well as expanding their growth of creative thinking (Schurgin O'Keeffe, 2011) and open mindedness to the world as a whole because they are accessible to all the information in the snap of a finger. One source has indicated that the usage of Facebook and other social media platforms have given shy children a virtual platform, which can soon extend to face-to-face interactions (Trapp, 2016). I believe that most adolescents use social media sometimes to improve their "offline relationships" when they are unable to strengthen them in the real-world. This socialization that adolescents tend to face through social media platforms improves their social circles because as teenagers engage in building new connections in the virtual world, they can furthermore be easily adapted to meet people, in the real-world, with a more pleasant encounter.

3.3. ENHANCED LEARNING

Social Media can also improve enhanced learning skills amongst young adults by enabling a wide range of possibilities in learning newer information. Let's say a teen has queries about a subject they learnt in class, or even if is about a general theory that they want to inquire and learn more information about, social media can be a considerate tool in aiding them to find helpful pages and solutions online that can help them seamlessly find the response to their questions without always going and asking someone (White, 2019). In this social space, they get information from skilled applicants who may have a greater experience on the scope of research. Also, due to enhanced learning capabilities, teenagers can develop more skills by using social media, making themselves more capable in getting jobs in the future, or even helping them earn themselves, just by not gaining skills but also sharing various methods and approaches based on the research topic. Most parents can thus identify the trend in their learning behaviors and development in their cognitive skills, through social media exploration towards learning approaches.

3.4. TEENS AND SELF-ESTEEM

Most teens feel isolated in their social circles and sometimes it is exceedingly difficult for a parent or a real-life friend to drag them out. Based on the analysis of the survey results that I have collected for to test the self-esteem levels of the teenaged students, I can conclude that as teenagers tend to use social media for a higher amount of time than average, it tends to result in most teens having a higher confidence and satisfaction level in themselves through their usage. The data is shown on the graphs below.

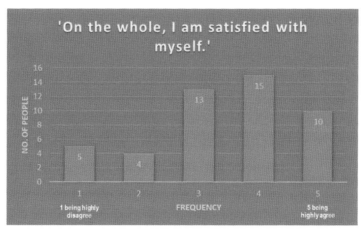

Chart 3: Result on Satisfaction of Usage of Social Media
(Students Perspective)

In this graph, we can identify how students are mostly satisfied with their social media usage. This indicates the positive link of social media usage to their personal lives, and how they are well pleased with its usage.

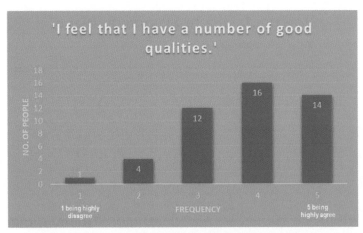

Chart 4: Students Perspectives on their confidence levels, due to social media usage

This graph shows how students perceive that they have good qualities despite their usage of social media, and this indicated how they are affirmed to having a higher self-esteem due to their usage, making more confident through their usage.

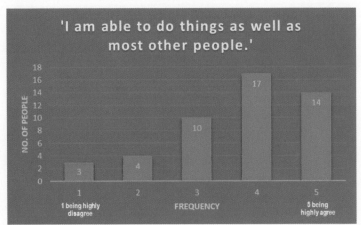

Chart 5: Result on Confidence Levels due to social media usage (Students' perspectives)

This graph shows how students link their social media usage to their ability of confidently achieving and doing things in life. The majority of students agree of having a higher confidence level due to their usage of social media, enabling them to be being satisfied in life.

Social media platforms such as YouTube or TikTok, gives young millennials a better sense of content or satisfaction in their lives. A survey done by Defy Media interpreted that 62% of the young millennial Americans, tend to like digital media usage because it makes them "feel good" (Stone, 2015). There are many reasons that induce these young millennials to endure this feeling. Firstly, they want to openly show off their talent to a widened community range. This will help them increase their self-confidence whilst sharing their perspectives or talents in front of a camera, and also will allow them to stand up and share media openly, unlike in the real-world, where at most times, it is considered more or less as a one-time opportunity. Secondly, when teens usually spend their time on social media platforms such as YouTube, they tend to watch various vloggers not only for entertainment purposes but also to gain various recommendations and advices about a specific theme. Taking the example of Bethany Mota, a 24 year-old YouTube star, having over 10 million subscribers on YouTube, we can identify how, when she releases a new beauty life hack or recommends a new beauty product, many teen communities who comprise of her followers tend to go try it out (STRASBURGER, 2015). Most teenagers set reminders to see when their favorite Youtubers or creators upload their new videos every week to stay on track or updated with the latest content.

IV. Negative impacts of social media

Social media is considered as one of the greatest improvements of mankind, throughout the years, to facilitate communication between people around the world. However, despite its positive effects on young people's mental health, it is considered to occupy more space in their daily lives, and thus, negative effects are shadowed by its usage. The positive effects might be visualizing to a person's conscience, but we should also consider the negative effects of social media on young people's mental health, and how it is negatively impacting their lives, as the future, can be predicted with a continuous usage of social medias.

Based on the questionnaire results given to students and teachers, the majority identifies social media addiction as the main negative effects that social media brings to the mental health of teenagers. The data is presented in the graphs below.

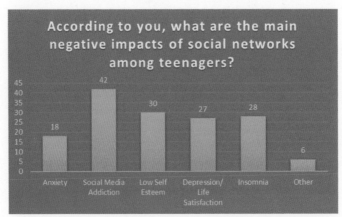

**Chart 6: Main negative effect of social Media usage
(Students Perspectives)**

In this graph, it can be identified, that according to the students that took part of this questionnaire, most of them had affirmed of the fact that social media addiction, seemed to be the main negative effect of social media usage.

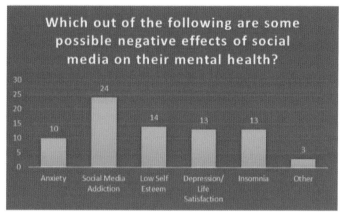

Chart 7: Main negative effect of social Media usage (Teachers Perspectives on Students)

In this graph, along with the students' graph, it can be said that even the teachers perceive that the main effect of social media on young people's mental health is social media addiction.

Most modern-day adolescents have taken the usage of social medias, as an advantage, to high extents without any restriction on its usage boundaries, and this poses a serious threat to their well-beings (Prajapati, 2019), both knowingly and unknowingly. Social media is often tied in with the notion of being more addictive than cigarettes and alcohols amongst young adults (Zhukova, 2018). Young adults can be classified as digital natives, a term originated by Mark Prensky in 2001, to describe the current generation of individuals who evolved in the era of ubiquitous technology, including social medias and the internet (HALTON, 2019).

4.1. SOCIAL MEDIA AND DEPRESSION

A previous study on the association of the usage of Social Networking Sites(SNS) and Insomnia, and Depression among Japanese Adolescents, confirmed that 2 hours or more a day spent on the usage of mobile phones, for activities such as SNS and other online chat, could potentially increase risks of depression (Tamura, Nishida, Tsuji, & Sakakibara, 2017). SNS and other online chat applications, enables an individual to communicate and interact with a larger number of people, seamlessly, due to the mass connectivity of the internet. Hence, adolescents, and younger users spend more time on them.

Taking the example of Facebook, one of the well-known SNS, used amongst teenagers, out of the 1.62 billion people who use Facebook daily (Zephoria Digital Marketing, 2019), 113.3 million of its users, consists of teenagers aged from 13-17 (Li, n.d.). This is incredibly shocking because as an 8-year study states, the amount of time spent by adolescents on social networking sites has skyrocketed to 62.5 percent since 2012 and continues to rise (University, 2019).

According to a study done by the American Academy of Pediatrics (AAP) on the impact of social media on children, adolescents and families, "Facebook Depression" is a term developed by researchers, to define depression that is developed amongst teenagers and preteens, when they spend high amounts of time on SNSs and then begin to portray various symptoms of depression (Gwenn Schurgin O'Keeffe, 2011). This tends to affect the teenager vastly, because as they get depressed, in the real-world, they will not tend to act as normal, and may develop side effects either academically, or whilst having face-to-face talks with their parents, friends, or any other person. To summarize this, we can use the example from a quote by Brent L. Fletcher, LCSW, who is an outpatient mental health therapist, who said that "Facebook and other social medias may contribute to depression in three ways—bullying, comparison with others, and influencing self-worth" (Pelt, n.d.). This is totally agreeable because, kids tend to be depressed, when they get bullied often online, which is a commonly occurring phenomena. Based on personal experience, apps like Instagram, YouTube and TikTok allow its users to get several followers. When, young adults have followers, they compare it with the ones of their friends, and thus most adolescents tend to want to pass their friends, and set a new milestone, and "Become Popular". Also, when self-worth is concerned, higher amounts of SNS usage amongst the youth, can lead to an influence in their lives because as one action affects the others, negative comments can rapidly reduce their self-esteem levels, thus rapidly enabling depression levels to increase. If a teenager does not take heed of his or her usage of SNS platforms, social media depression can also lead to suicidal ideation due to effects such as cyberbullying, despite such cases being rare (O'Reilly, et al., 2018).

4.2. SOCIAL MEDIA AND ANXIETY

According to the American Psychology Association, Anxiety is defined as an emotion that is characterized by feelings of tension, worried thoughts and physical changes like increased blood pressure (American Psychological Association, n.d.). Most teens are largely connected to their smartphones and use social medias vastly. Due to this usage, they have a greater susceptibility of having a distinguished social acceptance along with a higher popularity with other friends across the globe. This then brings to the negative effect of social media on teenagers, named specifically as **FOMO- the Fear of Missing Out.** FOMO refers to the anxiety and discomfort that a person feels when they think they're missing out on fun experiences (SECURLY BLOG, 2019). Normally when teens have high amount of social media usage, this typically makes them have the tendency to be "addicted" to their devices. This will then lead to their full-time consciousness and mindset only on their smartphones or other mobile devices. A recent research had indicated that in 2012, only 41% young adults had a smartphone compared to the 89% of teens in 2018. However, 34% of those teens used SNSs, multiple times a day in 2012, compared to the 70% of teens in 2018 (Smart Social, 2019). These figures are incredibly shocking and thus portrays how teenagers are slowly getting addicted to social media sites, due to technological development, and thus negative effects are portrayed, along the way. Based on the questionnaire results that I had conducted for this research, amongst 50 students, most kids spend in between 3 to more than 5 hours on their smartphones every day.

This can be outlined on the graph below, showing how most of the inquired children tend to be using their smartphones for more than the average amount of times, indicated by 24-Hour Movement Guidelines that recreational screen time usage should be used by teenagers, which is 2 hours (Participation Co., 2018). If both the graphs below are compared, we can see that teenagers of the current generation are using social media more than teachers and this is because they become more prone to its usage.

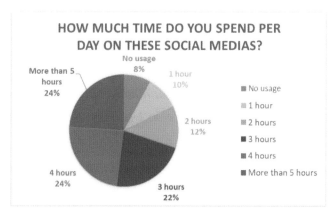

Chart 8: Students Results on Daily Social Media Usage

In this graph, it can be identified that 24% of the students that were questioned, say that they use social media daily for more than 5 hours daily.

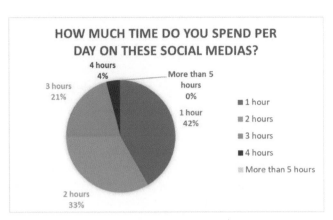

Chart 9: Teachers Results on Daily Social Media Usage

In this graph, that was given to teachers, it can be said that 42% of teachers use social media for 1 hour a day. When this data is compared to the one of the students, it is noticeable that the current young generation is more prone to social media usage than the older generations.

These statistics can help us understand how teenagers' irresistible desire to connect with SNSs and to share posts, affects them vastly, due to their constant check-in with new updates or posts. Many researches have proven that teenagers spend more time on their smartphones, online, in a virtual world, rather than interacting in the real-world.

A CNN report delved into the ways how social media is directly affecting teenagers' mental health, by making them more distressed and other factors influencing their mental health (Hadad, 2015). After their research, they have concluded that the heaviest social media users acknowledged to checking their social media feeds more than 100 times a day, sometimes even during school hours. When teens are usually not using their mobile devices, they feel anxious about what is going on online, and that is what normally leads to uncontrollable checking of their mobile devices, and increased levels of anxiety.

4.3. SOCIAL MEDIA AND INSOMNIA

According to the National Sleep Foundation, Insomnia can be defined as the difficulty of falling asleep even when an individual has the chance to do so. Its symptoms in normal young adults include fatigue due to low energy, a higher difficulty in concentration, mood disturbances, increasing their potential stress levels and reduced performance levels at school or at workplaces *(National Sleep Foundation, n.d.)*. An adequate sleep is needed for all teens because as they are growing, and their bodies are developing to the adult stage. Research has shown that teens should get about 8 to 10 hours of sleep to properly function properly *(National Sleep Foundation, n.d.)*. However, science has shown that sleep hormone levels (melatonin levels) in teenage blood usually rise during nighttime and drops in the morning *(NIMH, n.d.)*. This also explains why most teenagers, like me, stay up late at night, and struggle to wake up early in the morning to go to school.

A previous study done to find the usage of mobile phone and SNSs among Japanese adolescents noted that the usage of 5h or more had a higher risk of insomnia and sleep disturbances *(Tamura, Nishida, Tsuji, & Sakakibara, 2017)*. This clearly helps us understand how the excessive usage of social media platforms can affect an adolescent's mental health negatively, by causing strain to their brains every day, due to poor sleep and bad management of social media usage. When most kids are prone to insomnia, they usually tend to be having poorer sleep qualities, and this at most cases is due to their usage of social media before sleeping.

When young adults tend to use social medias every day, they are brought forth with the high levels of blue light that are emitted by the mobile and computer screens, which they use for viewing and thus impacts their circadian rhythms *(Walton, 2019)*. This blue light produces melatonin in their bodies, that not only makes them distracted from sleeping but also can stop them from feeling sleepy throughout the night at all *(Strickland, 2014)*. The big question is why teens want to increase their time limits using social media. Well the answer is simple. Most teens, as previously said, have the fear of missing out (FOMO), and that is why we can see most of them checking their smartphones every 2 minutes, to get instantaneously updated.

Personally, I think that teenagers should have to restrict their social media usage and concentrate on having a better sleep routine, as per the average, indicated by researchers, so that they have a proper functional mental health. Experts have suggested that to start solving this addictive usage of social media amongst teenagers, they should try to avoid using social media or other activities in front of any screen, at least one hour before sleeping *(Walton, 2019), (Hale, 2018)*.

4.4. SOCIAL MEDIA AND SELF-ESTEEM

Self- Esteem is usually associated with the phenomena of feeling good about oneself, or how a person perceives about themselves. Teenagers usually want to derive the fact that the usage of social media platforms will give them a better feeling. However, as teenagers indulge in the usage of social media platforms every day, their self-esteem levels tend to decrease. This is usually because of social comparisons, which happens, because teens are prone to compare themselves, superior to others with either potential positive or negative characteristics *(New York Behavioral Health, n.d.)*.

One study investigated the impact of Instagram, on the body image of young girls, to compare their appearances with the ones of other attractive models, thus putting themselves in a bad mood, leading to side effects such as eating disorders. Some teens fail to understand that most attractive pictures on social networks are photoshopped to make them look like the "perfect" individual. The previous research also proves how such comparison leads to women leading to body dissatisfaction and depression *(Fardouly, Pinkus, & Vartanian, 2016)*. This usually happens with young teenage girls, because they usually tend to perceive the notions of becoming like their online icons, or famous people that they usually try to mimic or admire.

Most adolescents also relate their social media usage to their sense of self-worth of followers, like or comments that they receive on a site. Naomi Smart, a YouTube Channel, informs her audience on her opinion on how "Instagram isn't always real", and how no one is perfect, even if people tend to change their body styles on Instagram posts to seem like they are perfect, through the editing process of those specific posts, and thus describes how it reduces self-esteem instantaneously *(Smart, Naomi, 2019)*. From this source, one can clearly identify how important it is to reduce social media usage amongst teens, because most teens are prone to this phenomena of feeling "jealous or envious" about other users, who at most times are not real, and try all their best to "become as perfect as they look", or even by gaining a maximum amount of likes and followers on their accounts, thus causing changes and affecting their self-esteem and their overall lives.

Another research survey that was carried out to find the relationship between Social Media Addiction and Self-Esteem amongst University Students, showed that as the levels of social media usage increases, the level of life satisfaction amongst the students decreased. This clearly means that according to the study, there is a negative correlation between social media usage and self-esteem. *(Hawi & Samaha, 2016)*. However, based on the questionnaire results that were gathered for this research, many teen-aged students have good confidence level and are proud of what they are doing. This can indicate that not all teenagers feel the same about the change in their self-esteem levels due to social media usage.

So, by taking care of the negative impacts of social media, we should maintain a proper mental and confidence level of today's youth. Also, most teenage individuals appear to have more positive views about themselves, when they have a higher self-esteem, whereas, the ones who have a lower self-esteem status, usually tend to be either being unsure of having negative considerations of their self-worth (Trifiro, 2018).

V. Conclusion

Social Media can be characterized in many ways, mostly based on its impacts on the mental health of adolescents'. As the research question aimed to investigate the extent at which social media impacts the mental health of the youth, it can be concluded that social media usage amongst teens is usually associated with its negative effects rather than its positive effects, and this is why most teens should take heed of their daily media usage, to help reduce the potential associated negative effects that it brings to their mental health.

The positive effects of social media on young people's phycological well-being are amongst a wide range. The usage of social media positively impacts empathy in teens giving them a better sense of support for their selves, and for others, as well as helps to offer a confidence boost in their lives, examples including marginalized communities, that are looking for a virtual community to help them vividly express themselves, without any boundaries. Social Media usage indisputably impacts socialization and communication by improving teenagers' encounters with other individuals, as they are prone to be more openminded to world topics and thus logically act on their situations to move from being shy to having communications in the virtual world through SNSs and finally open to face-to-face social interactions with others in the real-world. In this situation, communication is strengthened, and relationships are widened. Social Media usage also increments enhanced learning facilities in adolescents by helping them develop more skills as well as to increase their cognitive learning. Its usage also helps teens to feel more positive about themselves by having a better sense of satisfaction or even self-confidence in their lives, whilst sharing an idea or talent.

There are many negative effects associated with the usage of social media amongst teens, and this can skeptically affect the mental health of the adolescents that tend to be faced with its demerits. Its impact on increasing levels of depression is that it can lead to symptoms such as not acting normally, academic stress, or in other cases whilst having face-to-face talks with people in the real world, and they will tend to have a lesser mood. Also, some sources say that increased levels of depression due to social media usage can lead to suicidal ideation, despite such cases being rare. Social Media has an increasing impact on anxiety because as social media usage increases, more people are prone to the phenomena of FOMO- the Fear of Missing Out, thus leading to regular checking, and guarding a temporary mindset on social media applications. Adolescents are also affected by Insomnia, by having lower levels of sleep qualities because due to the excessive checking of their devices, they are prone to the blue light that is emitted, that causes strain as well as poor sleep management. However, social media tends to impact self-esteem levels drastically, because as teenagers increase their usage levels, their self-esteem levels decreases because they vastly consider the concept of "self-worth" and compares themselves to their social friends, which can thus lead to side effects like jealously and depression.

The negative effects outweigh the positive effects, and this can be a problem. This can be proved through the questionnaire results, which indicate that students use social media more than teachers and can thus have a widened impact on their lives.

Therefore, some recommendations are supposed to be put in place, to ensure that the potential negative effects of social media are reduced.

- Parents, can help their children (teenagers), to try newer outdoor activities, that spark their confidence levels, rather than activities on computers or mobile devices, and as they feel good about what they aim to do, they tend to become happier, and achieve more success in their lives, thus increasing their self-esteem levels *(Ehmke, n.d.)*. To achieve this, parents should constantly check on their children and introduce them into a technology-free environment.

- As previously said, teenagers need to evict the usage of social media at least thirty minutes to one hour before sleeping *(Grové, 2017)*, to reduce the potential harm of insomnia, and stress levels as well as the thought of social media activity during sleep.

- Whilst studying or do any academic activities, teenagers should avoid the usage of social media at least by one hour, because the social media content, will mix up with what they are studying or doing, and thus, distorting their minds, which can lead to problems of concentration.

- Based on previous studies, I can affirm that teenagers should not use social media applications for more than 2 hours a day *(Tamura, Nishida, Tsuji, & Sakakibara,*

2017). This will help reduce the potential effects related to depression and anxiety. To achieve this limited timespan, teenagers, can put their phones on the "Do not Disturb Mode", by silencing notifications, or even switching off their phones if necessary, to help staying focused, and avoid social media usage through checking their mobile phones excessively. Keeping a schedule for each day, is necessary for ensuring that social media usage in limited for a specific timeframe per day.

- Parents should help teenagers when they encounter problems on social media, such as depression due to posts that decrease their mood. Thus, they should unfollow all the accounts that they feel uncomfortable with, to avoid any form of social problems that can severely affect their mental health.

- Adolescents should be prone to not releasing their personal information online, because it can help avoid social bullying between the teen and other accounts and can help parents typically reduce the effect that social media usage by their children has on their mental health.

- Deleting the social media applications that are not being used. This can avoid opening the app after every two minutes, directly after getting a notification. The advantage of deleting some selected apps such as Facebook, is that by following this recommendation, the teenager can open the app on the web, when he/she would like to chat or urgently check an information, without opening the app each time *(Marvin, 2019).*

- Teenagers should engage in spending their free time properly. They should do many activities such as spending time with family, going outside to take a walk, playing board games, etc., and actively engaging themselves in the real-world, by avoiding all possible screens.

- Adolescents should practice self-control techniques to reduce the impact that their addiction has on their mental health. To achieve this, they can carry out mediation, and other self-healing techniques along with practicing Yoga, to relax their mental states and control themselves to a calmer mindful state of both body and mind.

BIBLIOGRAPHY

American Psychological Association. (n.d.). *Anxiety*. Retrieved January 20, 2020, from American Psychological Association: https://www.apa.org/topics/anxiety/

DOLLARHIDE, M. E. (2019, May 2). *Social Media Definition*. Retrieved November 3, 2019, from Investopedia: https://www.investopedia.com/terms/s/social-media.asp

Ehmke, R. (n.d.). *How Using Social Media Affects Teenagers*. Retrieved February 23, 2020, from Child Mind: https://childmind.org/article/how-using-social-media-affects-teenagers/

Facebook Investor Relations. (n.d.). *Facebook Investor Relations*. Retrieved November 3, 2019, from FAQs: https://investor.fb.com/resources/default.aspx

Fardouly, J., Pinkus, R. T., & Vartanian, L. R. (2016, December 19). *Instagram feeds do more damage to body image than billboards: study*. Retrieved February 1, 2020, from The Sydney Morning Herald: https://www.smh.com.au/lifestyle/social-media-shots-affect-body-image-because-we-only-show-our-best-side-20161219-gtdsa7.html

Garfield, S. (2014). Mind Change: How Digital Technologies Are Leaving Their Mark On Our Brains. New York: Penguin Random House UK. Retrieved January 10, 2020

Grové, C. (2017, December 7). *How parents and teens can reduce the impact of social media on youth well-being*. Retrieved February 23, 2020, from The Conversation: http://theconversation.com/how-parents-and-teens-can-reduce-the-impact-of-social-media-on-youth-well-being-87619

Gwenn Schurgin O'Keeffe, K. C.-P. (2011, April 1). Clinical Report—The Impact of Social Media on Children, Adolescents, and Families. *The Impact of Social Media on Children, Adolescents, and Families*, 127 (4) 800-804. doi:https://doi.org/10.1542/peds.2011-0054

Hadad, C. (2015, October 13). *Why some 13-year-olds check social media 100 times a day*. Retrieved January 21, 2020, from CNN Health: https://edition.cnn.com/2015/10/05/health/being-13-teens-social-media-study/

Hale, L. K.-D. (2018). *Youth screen media habits and sleep: sleep-friendly screen behavior recommendations for clinicians, educators, and parents*. Retrieved February 2, 2020, from Child and Adolescent Psychiatric Clinics: https://www.ncbi.nlm.nih.gov/pmc/articles/PMC5839336/

HALTON, C. (2019, July 15). *Digital Native*. Retrieved January 18, 2020, from Investopedia: https://www.investopedia.com/terms/d/digital-native.asp

Hawi, N. S., & Samaha, M. (2016, August 10). The Relations Among Social Media Addiction, Self-Esteem, and Life Satisfaction in University Students. *Sage Journals, 35* (5). doi:https://doi.org/10.1177/0894439316660340

Jacewicz, N. (2017, October 7). *Social media bad for the minds of young people, right? Maybe not*. Retrieved January 18, 2020, from USA Today: https://www.usatoday.com/story/money/2017/10/07/social-media-bad-minds-young-people-right-maybe-not/738820001/

Li, H. (n.d.). *Facebook and Zuckerberg keep getting 'freedom of expression' wrong*. Retrieved January 18, 2020, from TNW Podium: https://thenextweb.com/podium/2020/01/18/facebook-and-zuckerberg-keep-getting-freedom-of-expression-wrong/

Marvin, R. (2019, May 18). *How to Wean Yourself Off Smartphones and Social Media*. Retrieved February 24, 2020, from Pc Mag: https://www.pcmag.com/how-to/how-to-wean-yourself-off-smartphones-and-social-media

National Sleep Foundation. (n.d.). *Teens and Sleep*. Retrieved February 2, 2020, from SleepFoundation.org: https://www.sleepfoundation.org/articles/teens-and-sleep

National Sleep Foundation. (n.d.). *What is Insomnia?* Retrieved February 2, 2020, from SleepFoundation.org: https://www.sleepfoundation.org/insomnia/what-insomnia

New York Behavioral Health. (n.d.). *New York Behavioral Health*. Retrieved February 2, 2020, from Social Media Use and Self-Esteem: https://newyorkbehavioralhealth.com/social-media-use-and-self-esteem

NIMH. (n.d.). *MENTAL HEALTH INFORMATION: The Teen Brain: 6 Things to Know*. Retrieved February 2, 2020, from National Institute of Mental Health: https://www.nimh.nih.gov/health/publications/the-teen-brain-6-things-to-know/index.shtml

O'Reilly, M., Dogra, N., Whiteman, N., Hughes, J., Eruyar, S., & Reilly, P. (2018, May 20). Is social media bad for mental health and wellbeing? Exploring the perspectives of adolescents. *SAGE Journals, 23*(4). doi:https://doi.org/10.1177/1359104518775154

PACIFIC STANDARD STAFF. (2016, May 25). *CAN FACEBOOK FOSTER ADOLESCENTS' EMPATHY?* Retrieved May 18, 2020, from Pacific Standard: https://psmag.com/news/can-facebook-foster-adolescents-empathy

Participation Co. (2018, March 13). *How much screen time is too much for teens?* Retrieved February 16, 2020, from PARTICIPACTION: https://www.participaction.com/en-ca/blog/how-much-screen-time-is-too-much-for-teens

Pelt, J. V. (n.d.). *Is 'Facebook Depression' For Real?* Retrieved January 20, 2020, from Social Network Today Web Exclusive: https://www.socialworktoday.com/archive/exc_080811.shtml

Prajapati, V. (2019, June 10). *The Negative Effects of Social Media on Teenagers, Youth or Adolescents*. Retrieved January 18, 2020, from Techprevue: https://www.techprevue.com/negative-social-media-adolescents/

Schurgin O'Keeffe, G. &.-P. (2011). Clinical Report-The Impact of Social Media on Children, Adolescents, and Families. *Pediatrics (Evanston)* , 800-804. Retrieved February 2, 2020, from https://pediatrics.aappublications.org/content/pediatrics/early/2011/03/28/peds.2011-0054.full.pdf

SECURLY BLOG. (2019, May 17). *The Link Between Social Media and FOMO in Teenagers*. Retrieved January 21, 2020, from SECURLY BLOG: https://blog.securly.com/2019/05/17/the-link-between-social-media-and-fomo-in-teenagers/

Smart Social. (2019, October 23). *Teen Social Media Statistics 2019 (What Parents Need to Know)*. Retrieved January 21, 2020, from Smart Social: https://smartsocial.com/social-media-statistics/

Smart, Naomi. (2019, March 3). Is Instagram Lowering Your Self Esteem? #SmartChats. Retrieved February 1, 2020, from https://www.youtube.com/watch?v=EhYZRKN1e5Q

Social Media Use Increases Empathy For Peers. (2016, July 7). Retrieved January 18, 2020, from BiteScience Communcation and Media: https://bitescience.com/articles/social-media-use-increases-empathy-for-peers/

Stone, M. (2015, March 3). *Teens love YouTube because it makes them feel good about themselves, a new survey says*. Retrieved February 2, 2020, from Business Insider:

https://www.businessinsider.com/teens-love-youtube-because-it-makes-them-feel-good-about-themselves-2015-3

⊗ STRASBURGER, C. (2015, March 3). *Say What? Turns Out YouTube Is Actually Making Teens Feel BETTER About Themselves*. Retrieved February 2, 2020, from teenVogue: https://www.teenvogue.com/story/youtube-teen-confidence-booster

⊗ Strickland, A. (2014). Exploring the Effects of Social Media Use on the. *University of Central Florida*. Retrieved from https://stars.library.ucf.edu/honorstheses1990-2015/1684

⊗ Tamura, H., Nishida, T., Tsuji, A., & Sakakibara, H. (2017). Association between Excessive Use of Mobile Phone and Insomnia and Depression among Japanese Adolescents. *International Journal of Environmental Research and Public Health*, 14(7). doi:701. doi:10.3390/ijerph14070701

⊗ Thoughtful Learning. (2014). *Thoughtful Learning: Inquire*. Retrieved January 18, 2020, from The Purpose of Social Media: http://thoughtfullearning.com/inquireHSbook/pg271

⊗ Trapp, K. (2016, June 27). *Effects of Facebook on Teenagers: Positive and Negative*. Retrieved February 2, 2020, from WeHaveKids: https://wehavekids.com/parenting/Teens-and-Facebook

⊗ Trifiro, B. (2018). Instagram Use and It's Effect on Well-Being and Self-Esteem. *Master of Arts in Communication*(Paper 4). Retrieved February 1, 2020, from https://digitalcommons.bryant.edu/macomm/4

⊗ University, B. Y. (22, October 18). *Overall time on social media is not related to teen anxiety and depression: Eight-year study shows screen time isn't the problem*. Retrieved January 18, 2020, from ScienceDaily: www.sciencedaily.com/releases/2019/10/191022174406.htm

⊗ Verywell Mind. (2019, November 27). *Importance and Benefits of Empathy*. Retrieved November 2019, 18, from Verywell Mind: https://www.verywellmind.com/what-is-empathy-2795562

⊗ Walton, A. G. (2019, October 24). *Social Media Use May Mess With Teens' Sleep*. Retrieved February 2, 2020, from Forbes: https://www.forbes.com/sites/alicegwalton/2019/10/24/heavy-social-media-use-may-steal-teens-sleep/#3cd5d90669bf

⊗ White, L. (2019). *Positive Effects of Social Media on Teenagers*. Retrieved February 2, 2020, from Relation Advisors: https://relationadvisors.com/positive-effects-of-social-media-on-teenagers/

⊗ Zephoria Digital Marketing. (2019, October 30). *The Top 20 Valuable Facebook Statistics – Updated January 2020*. Retrieved Janurary 18, 2020, from Zephoria Digital Marketing: https://zephoria.com/top-15-valuable-facebook-statistics/

⊗ Zhukova, A. (2018, October 31). *7 Negative Effects of Social Media on People and Users*. Retrieved February 2, 2020, from MakeUseOf: https://www.makeuseof.com/tag/negative-effects-social-media/ \

APPENDIX

QUESTIONNAIRE OF THE IMPACT OF SOCIAL MEDIA ON TEENAGERS' MENTAL HEALTH

1. Do you use Social Media?
- Yes
- No

Effect of Social Media Usage

2. (If yes, which ones do you use the most?)
- SNAPCHAT
- INSTAGRAM
- FACEBOOK
- TWITTER
- LINKEDIN
- TIKTOK
- WHATSAPP
- YOUTUBE
- OTHER:

3. How much time do you spend per day on these social medias?

- 1 hour
- 2 hours
- 3 hours
- 4 hours
- 5 hours
- More than 5 hours

4. On a scale of 1 to 5, do you think that social media is positively impacting

   teenagers/young people?

	1	2	3	4	5	
Highly Disagree	◯	◯	◯	◯	◯	Strongly Agree

5. According to you, what are the main positive impacts of social networks among teenagers? (Select as much answers necessary)
- To keep in touch with family, relatives, and friends
- To find out latest news
- To share personal photos and videos through experiences
- For research work
- To get a relief from academic stress
- To become more sociable by creating a social identity
- Other

6. On a scale of 1 to 5, do you think that social media is negatively impacting teenagers/young people's lives'?

	1	2	3	4	5	
Highly Disagree	○	○	○	○	○	Strongly Agree

7. Which out of the following are some possible negative effects of social media on their mental health? (Select as much answers necessary)
- Anxiety
- Social Media Addiction
- Low Self Esteem
- Depression / Life satisfaction
- Insomnia
- Other:

Social Media and Me! (This part is only for students)

8. On a scale of 1 to 5, rate your usage of social media.

	1	2	3	4	5	
I am not active on any social media networks	○	○	○	○	○	I am one of the most active students on social media networks

9. On the whole, I am satisfied with myself.

	1	2	3	4	5	
Highly Disagree	○	○	○	○	○	Strongly Agree

10. At times, I think I am no good at all.

	1	2	3	4	5	
Highly Disagree	○	○	○	○	○	Strongly Agree

11. I feel that I have a number of good qualities.

	1	2	3	4	5	
Highly Disagree	○	○	○	○	○	Strongly Agree

12. I am able to do things as well as most other people.

	1	2	3	4	5	
Highly Disagree	○	○	○	○	○	Strongly Agree

13. I feel like I do not have much to be proud of in life.

	1	2	3	4	5	
Highly Disagree	○	○	○	○	○	Strongly Agree

Printed in Great Britain
by Amazon

36809174R00027